Little People, **BIG DREAMS**®

BOB DYLAN

Written by
Maria Isabel Sánchez Vegara

Illustrated by
Conrad Roset

Frances Lincoln
Children's Books

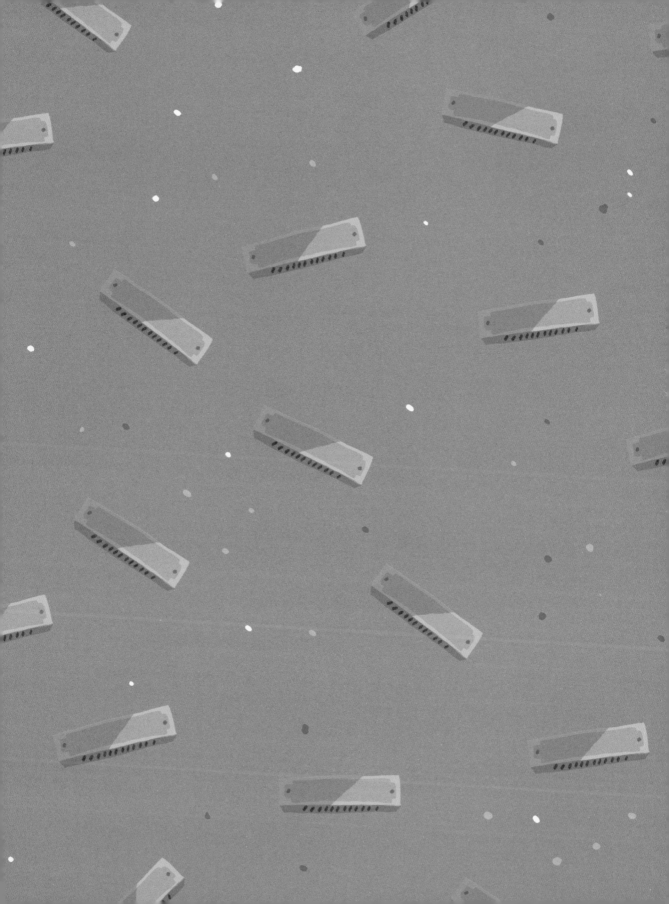

Growing up in Hibbing, America, wasn't very exciting for little Robert, the eldest son of the Zimmermans. He liked to listen to music on the radio and imagine he was somewhere else...

Inspired by his rock idols, Robert taught himself the guitar, the harmonica and a strange instrument called the autoharp, which he played to an audience that was easily pleased.

At school, Robert would rather be invisible than draw attention to himself. When he took part in a talent contest, the teacher turned his microphone off. Robert sounded like a dog whose leg was caught in barbed wire!

That didn't stop him. He experimented with rock, blues and country music. At college, he found his rhythm playing old folk songs. The simple tunes were written by ordinary people, who told stories about everyday life.

Robert soon started composing his own songs.
He had a real talent for writing rhymes and making
words fit to a beat. The songs were poetic yet powerful,
and he wrote them under his new name: Bob Dylan.

One year later, Bob dropped out of college and moved to New York. There, he was a nobody. But he had his guitar, his harmonica and another useful instrument: a hat. He was determined to use it, passing it around in bars where he played.

One day, a guy from a record company came to one of his gigs. He was impressed by Bob's raw force and fresh lyrics, and offered him his first music contract. Times were changing, and Bob's life was about to change, too.

Bob's music spoke about things that mattered: civil rights, war and religion. Without trying, he became the voice of a generation eager to change the world, putting down in words what millions of people felt.

His songs became anthems sung by the most amazing
artists of all times, reaching millions of people.
Many of them had not heard his voice
or known his name, but Bob didn't mind.

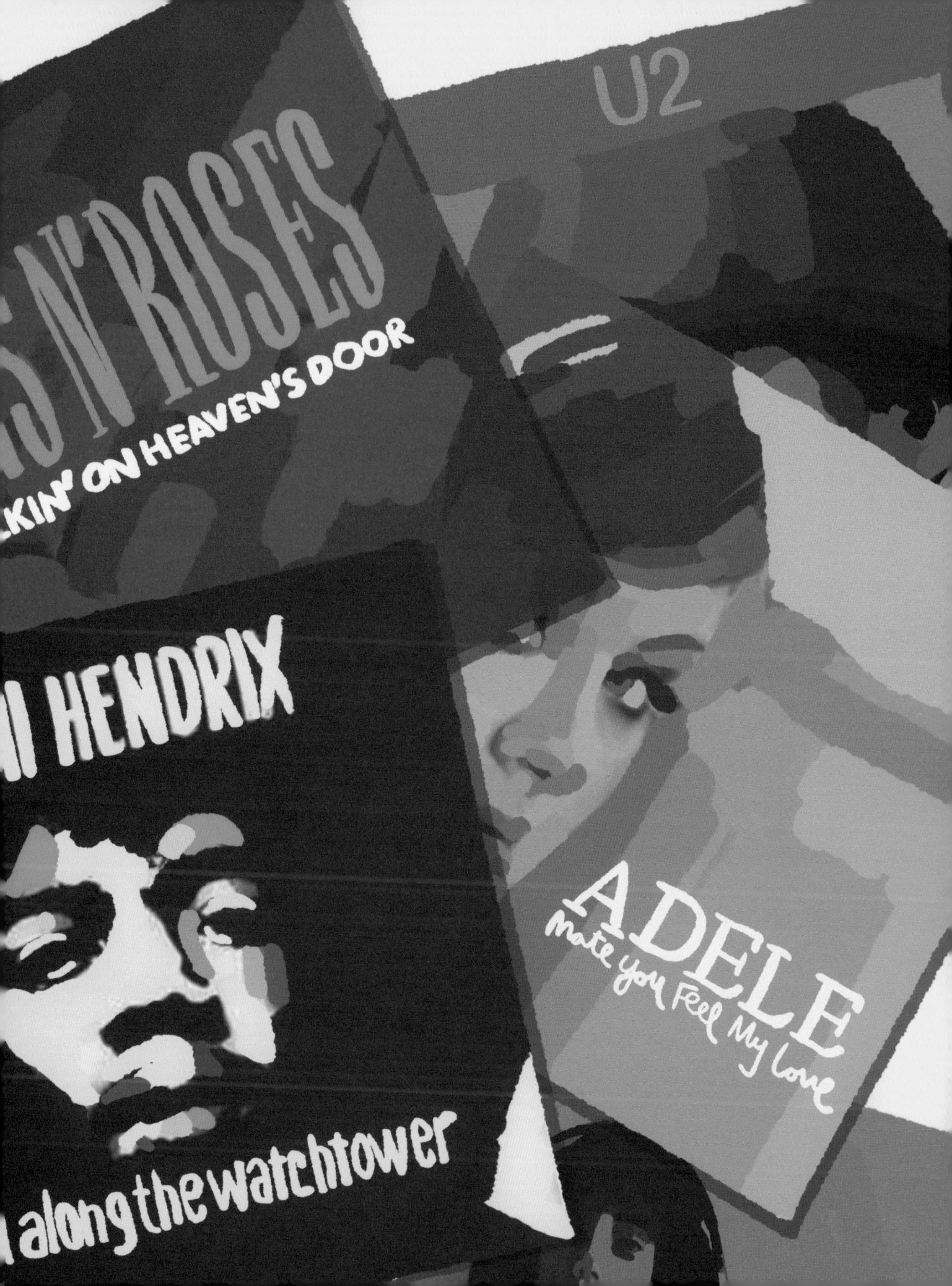

U2
N'ROSES
KIN' ON HEAVEN'S DOOR
HENDRIX
along the watchtower
ADELE
make you Feel My love

Instead of giving interviews or playing at being a star, Bob preferred to keep to himself. For him, a perfect day was working on a poem, riding around on his motorcycle or talking with friends.

Being an artist meant being free, and not caring about what others might think. Bob moved from folk to rock or pop, trying new sounds and exploring different styles, challenging himself as well as his fans.

He received all the awards an artist could dream of. And he was the first musician ever to be recognised with a Nobel Prize for Literature. But — in true Bob style — he didn't show up to the ceremony.

Today, little Bob – one of the greatest musicians and poets
of all time – feels cool just being himself.
He's an ordinary person who says what he thinks
and does what he likes most: writing songs.

BOB DYLAN

(Born 1941)

1961   1966

Born Robert Allen Zimmerman, Bob grew up with his little brother
and parents, Abram and Beatrice. Bob's grandparents emigrated
from Russia to the United States in 1905, and the family soon
became part of a close-knit Jewish community of Hibbing,
Minnesota. Bob's father Abram owned an electrical appliance shop,
and there Bob first listened to blues and country music stations, and
later, rock and roll. After several performances in the high school
band, Bob went to the University of Minneapolis, where he changed
his name and started to make folk music, which had 'more feeling
than rock and roll'. He soon dropped out of college and moved to
New York, where he met the famous Woody Guthrie and quickly

1975   2012

became his disciple. Befriending a community of folk musicians and supporting artists such as John Lee Hooker at shows, Bob soon became one of America's most promising young talents. Known not just for his performances, he was brilliant at writing songs that expressed what people felt and thought. He signed his first record deal aged 20 with Columbia Records, and quickly became known as one of the most original and poetic voices in popular music. Bob went on to win multiple awards for his contribution to music and literature, but his greatest achievement was simply 'being himself'. At a time of great change, Bob's music gave people a voice, and his work continues to do so for millions of listeners, young and old, today.

Want to find out more about **Bob Dylan?**

Have a read of this great book:

Forever Young by Bob Dylan and Paul Rogers

Brimming with creative inspiration, how-to projects, and useful information to enrich your everyday life, Quarto Knows is a favourite destination for those pursuing their interests and passions. Visit our site and dig deeper with our books into your area of interest: Quarto Creates, Quarto Cooks, Quarto Homes, Quarto Lives, Quarto Drives, Quarto Explores, Quarto Gifts, or Quarto Kids.

First published in the UK in 2020 by Frances Lincoln Children's Books, an imprint of The Quarto Group.
The Old Brewery, 6 Blundell Street, London N7 9BH, United Kingdom.
T (0)20 7700 6700 F (0)20 7700 8066 **www.QuartoKnows.com**
First Published in Spain in 2020 under the title Pequeño & Grande Bob Dylan
by Alba Editorial, s.l.u., Baixada de Sant Miquel, 1, 08002 Barcelona
www.albaeditorial.es
All rights reserved.

A catalogue record for this book is available from the British Library.
ISBN 978-0-7112-4674-4
eISBN 978-0-7112-4676-8

Set in Futura BT.

Published by Katie Cotton • Designed by Karissa Santos
Edited by Rachel Williams and Katy Flint • Production by Caragh McAleenan

Manufactured in Guangdong, China CC022021

9 7 5 3 4 6 8

Photographic acknowledgements (pages 28-29, from left to right) 1. Bob Dylan recording, 1961 © Michael Ochs Archives via Getty. 2. Bob Dylan, 1966 © Hulton Archive via Getty Images 3. Singer/Songwriter Bob Dylan performs, 1975 © Michael Ochs Archives via Getty. 4. US President Barack Obama presents the US Presidential Presidential Medal of Freedom to musician Bob Dylan during a ceremony on May 29, 2012 in the East Room of the White House in Washington , 2012 © AFP via Getty.

Collect the *Little People,* **BIG DREAMS**® series:

FRIDA KAHLO

COCO CHANEL

MAYA ANGELOU

AMELIA EARHART

AGATHA CHRISTIE

MARIE CURIE

ROSA PARKS

AUDREY HEPBURN

EMMELINE PANKHURST

ELLA FITZGERALD

ADA LOVELACE

JANE AUSTEN

GEORGIA O'KEEFFE

HARRIET TUBMAN

ANNE FRANK

MOTHER TERESA

JOSEPHINE BAKER

L. M. MONTGOMERY

JANE GOODALL

SIMONE DE BEAUVOIR

MUHAMMAD ALI

STEPHEN HAWKING

MARIA MONTESSORI

VIVIENNE WESTWOOD

MAHATMA GANDHI

DAVID BOWIE

WILMA RUDOLPH

DOLLY PARTON

BRUCE LEE

RUDOLF NUREYEV

ZAHA HADID

MARY SHELLEY

MARTIN LUTHER KING JR.

DAVID ATTENBOROUGH

ASTRID LINDGREN

EVONNE GOOLAGONG

BOB DYLAN

ALAN TURING

BILLIE JEAN KING

GRETA THUNBERG

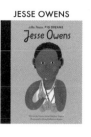

JESSE OWENS

JEAN-MICHEL BASQUIAT

ARETHA FRANKLIN

CORAZON AQUINO

PELÉ

ERNEST SHACKLETON

STEVE JOBS

AYRTON SENNA

LOUISE BOURGEOIS

ELTON JOHN

JOHN LENNON

PRINCE

CHARLES DARWIN

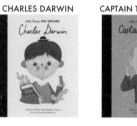

CAPTAIN TOM MOORE

HANS CHRISTIAN ANDERSEN

STEVIE WONDER

MEGAN RAPINOE

MARY ANNING

MALALA YOUSAFZAI

ANDY WARHOL

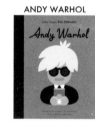

RUPAUL

ACTIVITY BOOKS

STICKER ACTIVITY BOOK

COLOURING BOOK

LITTLE ME, BIG DREAMS JOURNAL

Discover more about the series at www.littlepeoplebigdreams.co.uk

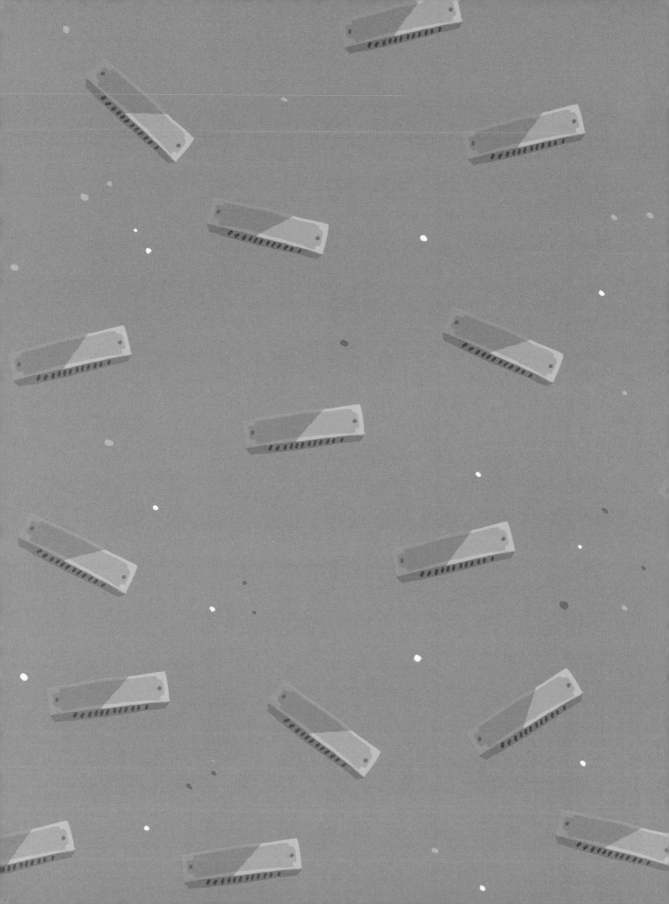